COOL SCIENCE

Experiments with Light and Color

By Tom Jackson

Gareth Stevens
Publishing

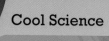

Introduction

Our planet is flooded with energy pouring out from the Sun. You can see things because this energy bounces off objects and into your eyes. This energy is called visible light, but there are invisible forms of solar energy. Together they are known as electromagnetic radiation.

Scientists have learned how to harness the energy in sunlight using solar panels. Solar power is a clean and green way to generate the electricity we need.

As the name suggests, visible light is the form of electromagnetic radiation that we can see. Light-sensitive cells at the back of our eyes detect the light rays bouncing off objects. The light-sensitive cells turn the light rays into tiny electrical signals, which pass along the optic nerves that lead from each eye to the brain. The brain then processes the electrical signals and creates a picture of the world around us.

Visible light is natural light from the Sun, but our eyes also see light from other sources. Some light comes from other stars in the sky. There are also street lamps and household lighting that we use to see in the dark.

But even these artificial lights get their energy from the Sun. When a lightbulb glows, it uses electricity that comes from burning fossil fuels such as oil and coal. Fossil fuels are the remains of animals and plants that lived millions of years ago. Plants use the energy from sunlight to make food and grow. Animals then eat plants. Scientists are even producing electricity directly using solar panels to capture the energy in sunlight.

Invisible radiation

Invisible forms of electromagnetic radiation include radio waves, microwaves, infrared light, ultraviolet light, X-rays, and gamma rays. All these forms of radiation are just like visible light, but they contain different amounts of energy. Although our eyes cannot see them, the invisible forms of radiation are still very useful. For example, doctors use X-rays to see inside the human body. Microwaves are used in the kitchen to cook our food. People send and receive messages around the world by bouncing radio waves off satellites in space.

Waves or particles?

Light has puzzled scientists for hundreds of years. In the seventeenth century, Dutch scientist Christiaan Huygens (1629–1695) suggested that light traveled in waves, just

LEARNING ABOUT SCIENCE

Doing experiments is the best way to learn about science. This is the way scientists test their ideas and find out new information. Follow this good science guide to get the most out of each experiment in this book.

• Never begin an experiment until you have talked to an adult about what you are going to do.
• Take care when you do or set up an experiment, whether it is dangerous or not. Make sure you know the safety rules before you start work. Wear goggles and use the right safety equipment when you are told to do so.
• Do each experiment more than once. The more times you carry out an experiment, the more accurate your results will be.
• Keep a notebook to record the results of your experiments. Make your results easy to read and understand. You can make notes and draw charts, diagrams, and tables.
• Drawing a graph is a great way of presenting your results. Plot the results of your experiment as dots on a graph. Use a ruler to draw a straight line through all the dots. Reading the graph will help you to fill in the gaps in your experiment.
• Write down the results as you do each experiment. If one result seems different from the rest, you might have made a mistake that you can fix immediately.
• Learn from your mistakes. Some of the most exciting findings in science came from an unexpected result. If your results do not tally with your predictions, try to find out why.

Bright lights from high-rise office blocks, street lamps, and automobiles light up the night sky in Singapore in Southeast Asia.

like ripples on a pond. English scientist Isaac Newton (1642–1727) did not agree. He noticed that light casts shadows with very sharp edges. Waves do not produce sharp edges—waves of water wash around objects and sound waves travel around corners. To explain the sharp edges of shadows, Newton suggested that light was a stream of tiny particles.

It took nearly two hundred years to get the answer. It turned out that all the scientists were right! Early in the twentieth century, German-born American physicist Albert Einstein (1879–1955) showed that light is made up of tiny particles of energy, called photons, that move like waves. In fact light does leak around objects, but Newton did not have a microscope powerful enough to see it. Einstein asked another important question about light. He wondered what you would see if you could travel on a beam of light. The answers Einstein came up with turned into his special theory of relativity, which was published in 1905. It stated that light always travels at exactly the same speed through empty space (see the box below).

Properties of light

The experiments in this book treat light as waves instead of particles. This branch of science is known as optics. Light waves behave like any other waves. They have a

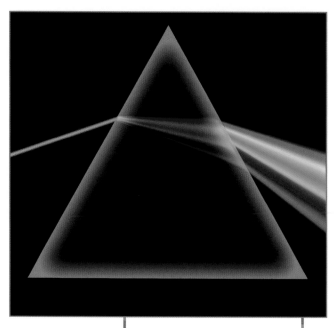

A prism splits white light into the seven colors of the rainbow.

wavelength (the distance between the peak of one wave and the next), amplitude (the height of the peak or trough), and a frequency (the number of waves produced every second). The experiments study some of the properties of waves, such as reflection (the way light bounces off objects) and refraction (the way light bends as it moves through objects).

Reflection

All objects reflect light. Smooth, shiny objects—such as a mirror and the surface of a still lake—produce the clearest reflections. A mirror makes light waves bounce in one direction only, producing very clear reflections. Shiny objects appear very bright. Light bounces off some objects in many different directions. This makes the surface of these objects look dull, and they do not produce clear reflections. Some objects actually absorb light. These objects appear black or a very dark color.

White light from the Sun is actually made up of the colors of the rainbow. Each color has a particular wavelength of light. The longest waves of visible light

SPEED OF LIGHT

Scientists have been trying to get an accurate figure for the speed of light for hundreds of years. The current estimate is around 186,000 miles (300,000 kilometers) per hour. This measurement is only an estimate, because the speed of light is measured in a vacuum—a space that contains absolutely nothing. Scientists cannot create a perfect vacuum to measure the speed of light, so the figure will always be slightly inaccurate. This is because the light slows down as it bounces off particles in the air.

are red; the shortest are violet. The different colors of white light are reflected by different amounts, and this gives an object its color. For example, a lemon looks yellow because it mostly reflects yellow light waves. The lemon absorbs all the other colors of white light.

Refraction

Light travels at different speeds through different substances. It travels fastest in empty space. It travels slower in air, slower still in water, and even slower in a solid such as glass. As light passes from one substance to another, it changes speed. So light slows down as it moves from the air into water or a glass prism. This bending process is called refraction. The different colors of white light bend by different amounts when they pass through different substances. If you shine white light into a prism, for example, it splits up into all the different colors of the spectrum. This is because violet light bends more than red light as it travels from the air into the glass. Rainbows form in exactly the same way, as sunlight passes through billions of raindrops.

Optical instruments

You can have lots of fun with light by making some of the instruments in the experiments in this book. You can make objects appear larger than life using a fishbowl lens (see pages 12–13) or view distant objects through a homemade telescope (see pages 16–17).

A rainbow forms when sunlight bounces off drops of rain and splits up into the seven colors: red, orange, yellow, green, blue, indigo, and violet.

Two-way Mirror

Goals

1 Make a two-way mirror.

2 Combine your face with another person's face.

LEVEL of Difficulty
 Hard   Medium   Easy

What you will need

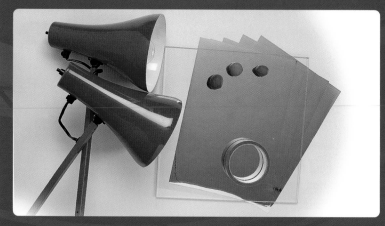

- 12-inch (30-cm) square piece of glass
- sheet of Mylar to cover the glass (ask for antiglare window film in a hardware store)
- cloth tape
- 2 electric lamps
- modeling clay
- assistant

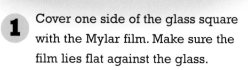

1 Cover one side of the glass square with the Mylar film. Make sure the film lies flat against the glass.

2 Use cloth tape to stick the film to the edge of the glass. Use more tape to cover the sharp edges of the glass.

3 Use pieces of modeling clay to stand the mirror upright on a tabletop. Make sure it is steady before you let go.

SUSPECT BEHAVIOR

Two-way mirrors are used when the victims of crimes are asked to identify a criminal in a police lineup. The lineup stands in front of a two-way mirror. The victim and police officers stand in a dark room on the other side of the mirror. The victim can see through the mirror to look at the people in the lineup. The victim cannot be seen by the suspect—as long as the viewing room is kept in darkness.

4 Put the lamps on the table, one on each side of the mirror. Close the drapes and turn out the lights to make the room as dark as possible. Ask a friend to sit opposite you on the other side of the mirror. Take turns switching the lamps on and off to illuminate your faces while you look at the mirror. Try it with one light at a time. Then try both lights on together.

TROUBLESHOOTING

What if I can't see through the two-way mirror?

Some Mylar sheets are thicker than others. It might also help to do this experiment at night so that you can make the room really dark. Make sure your faces are fully lit by the lamps. Try not to shine your lamp in the other person's face.

SAFETY TIP!

Cover the edges of the glass to prevent any accidental cuts.

Make a Rainbow

What you will need

- two 12-inch (30-cm) squares of Plexiglas about ⅛ inch (3 mm) thick
- clean cloth
- soap and water
- tape
- scissors
- piece of dark paper
- desk lamp

Goals

1 Create rainbow patterns of light.

2 Show that white light is made up of lots of different colors.

LEVEL of Difficulty   Hard   Medium   Easy

1 Clean both sides of the Plexiglas with soap and water. Rinse and dry the surfaces with a soft, clean cloth.

2 Press both Plexiglas squares together. Tape around the edges to hold them in place.

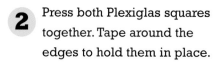

3 Tape the black paper to one side of the Plexiglas "sandwich."

TROUBLESHOOTING

What if I can't see any rainbow patterns?

If you cannot see colored patterns in the Plexiglas, separate the two sheets. Ask an adult to help you smear a thin layer of engine oil on one of the sheets. Tape the two sheets together, with the oil in the middle.

4 Hold the Plexiglas sandwich under a bright desk lamp, papered side down.

5 You should see patterns of different colors in the Plexiglas. These are caused by the light waves interfering with each other. Bend the Plexiglas. See how the patterns change.

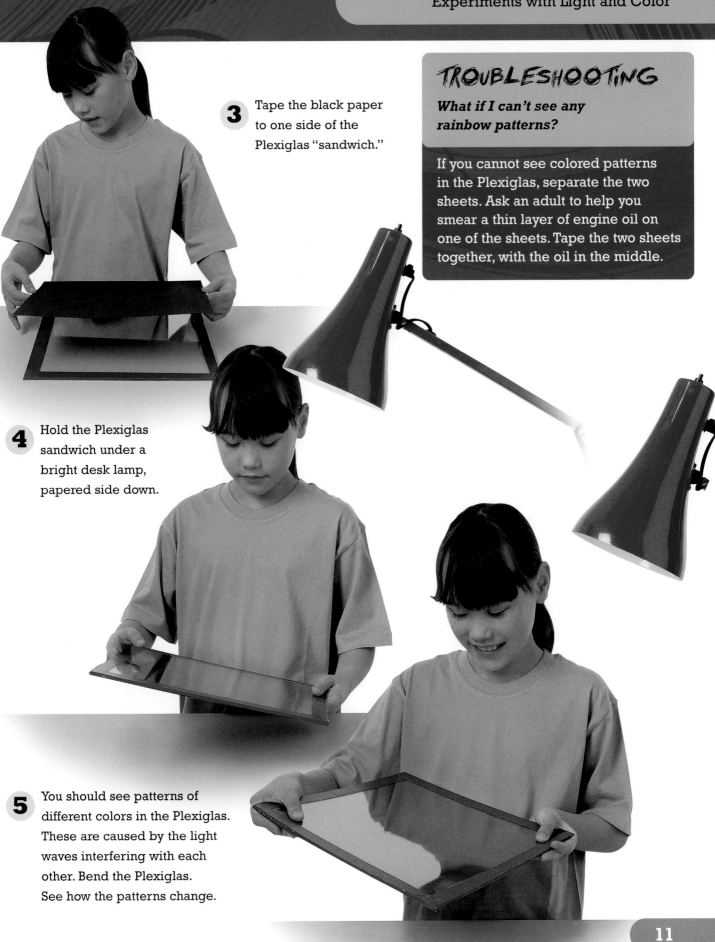

Fishbowl Lens

Goals

1 Create an image using a water lens.

2 Investigate how lenses work.

LEVEL of Difficulty

 Hard   Medium   Easy

What you will need

- glass bowl
- water
- candle
- dish
- piece of thick white card
- ruler

1 Fill the bowl with water. This will be your lens.

SAFETY TIP!

Keep the card well away from the candle flame at all times.

2 Place the candle on a dish about 12 inches (30cm) from the bowl. Ask an adult to light the candle for you.

LACEMAKER'S LENS

In the 18th century, lacemakers used water lenses to help them see as they sewed delicate patterns in clothes. Glass lenses were used to light fires by focusing light and heat from the Sun onto wood. Fires were sometimes started accidentally in this way.

Sometimes a room can be too bright. Sunlight can drown out the image of the candle. Try closing the drapes and turning out the lights to make the room darker. If the candle flame won't stop flickering, replace the candle with a small flashlight. Point the flashlight toward the bowl.

3 Hold the card on the other side of the water-bowl lens.

FUZZY IMAGE

The image formed by your fishbowl lens will probably be fuzzy, and the colors might overlap. The glass in the bowl bends the different colors of white light by different amounts. The separate colors occur because some colors of light bend more than others.

4 Gradually move the card away from the bowl. Stop when you see an image of the candle flame on the card. How does the image on the card compare to the flame itself?

Disappearing Trick

What you will need

- 2 glasses
- jug of water
- cooking oil
- baby oil
- 2 glass cocktail stirrers

Goals

1 See how different liquids slow down light.

2 Make a glass object disappear.

LEVEL of Difficulty

 Hard   Medium   Easy

1 Pour water into one glass until it is halfway full.

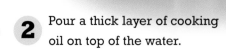

2 Pour a thick layer of cooking oil on top of the water.

FISHY BUSINESS

In some parts of the world fishers wade into the sea to catch fish one at a time with spears. Because of refraction, fish seen from above the water appear to be farther away than they really are, so the fishers compensate for this by aiming at a point that appears nearer than the fish.

TROUBLESHOOTING

What if the glass stirrers don't look faint in the oil?

The temperature of the oil and water affect the results in this activity. Try it on a cool day when the oil and water are much denser, and they bend the light more. If the liquids are too warm, cool the glasses in the fridge.

3 Fill half of the second glass with baby oil.

INVISIBLE ANIMALS

Sea animals, such as jellyfish and plankton, have see-through bodies, which bend light in the same way as the surrounding seawater. As a result, these animals are almost impossible to see, helping them to hide from predators.

4 Put the glass stirrers in the glasses. Look at the glasses from the side. What can you see? Are some parts of the stirrers fainter than others?

Make a Telescope

Goals

1 Make a refracting telescope.

2 Focus on a distant object.

LEVEL of Difficulty	Hard	Medium	Easy

What you will need

- Glass or plastic lenses
- 2 card tubes (one narrower than the other)
- tape

2 Rest the larger lens on one end of the larger card tube. Put a strip of tape around the end of the tube. Press it down gently to hold the lens in place.

1 Choose two lenses that are good at focusing on objects. Hold a small lens near to your eye and the large lens farther away. Use the lenses to focus on an object. Make sure that your card tubes are as long as the distance between the lenses.

3 Place the small lens on the end of the small tube. Tape it in place.

BINOCULARS

Binoculars are like two telescopes stuck together, with a telescope for each eye. Binoculars are better for judging distances than telescopes. The brain needs images from both eyes to figure out distances accurately.

4 Slide the open end of the small tube into the large tube. Choose an object at a distance. Try to bring it into focus by slowly moving the small tube in and out of the large tube.

TROUBLESHOOTING

My telescope doesn't focus very well.

Make sure the tubes fit together snugly. If they don't, the lenses won't stay lined up when you slide the tubes in and out. A steady hand also helps you to focus. Rest the end of your telescope on a piece of furniture or a window ledge.

SAFETY TIP!

Never use a telescope to look directly at the Sun or very bright lights. It could damage your eyes and may even blind you.

Trapped Beam

What you will need

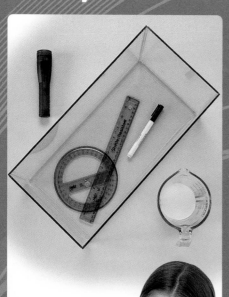

- glass tank full of water
- milk
- bright flashlight with a narrow beam
- washable felt-tip pen
- protractor
- assistant
- ruler

Goals

1 Trap a light beam in a tank of water.

2 Measure the critical angle for water.

LEVEL of Difficulty Hard Medium Easy

2 Shine the flashlight through the side of the tank. Angle the light beam so that it hits the surface of the water from below. Is the light reflected back through the water, or does it emerge into the air?

3 Move the flashlight so that the beam hits the surface at different angles. Can you find the critical angle? That is when the light beam travels along the surface.

1 Clean the tank. Fill it with water. Add a tiny bit of milk. You should still be able to see through the water clearly. Turn out the light, and close the drapes.

4 When you have found the critical angle, use a felt-tip pen to mark the beam's path with crosses on the front of the tank.

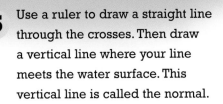

5 Use a ruler to draw a straight line through the crosses. Then draw a vertical line where your line meets the water surface. This vertical line is called the normal.

6 Use the protractor to measure the angle between the two lines. This is the critical angle for water.

Pinhole Camera

Goals

1 Make a pinhole camera.

2 Make images appear on a small screen.

LEVEL of Difficulty

 Hard   Medium   Easy

BIG AND SMALL

The very first cameras were pinhole cameras called camera obscuras. Some were the size of a whole room. Several people stood in the room to view a scene such as an eclipse of the Sun. Others were pocket-size models that artists used to help them paint a scene.

What you will need

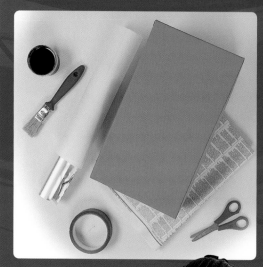

- shoebox
- paintbrush
- black paint
- newspaper
- scissors
- tape
- tracing paper
- aluminum foil
- pin

1 Paint the inside of the box black. Do not forget to paint the lid.

2 Cut out small squares at both ends of the box.

SAFETY TIP!

Take care when using scissors. Always cut away from your body.

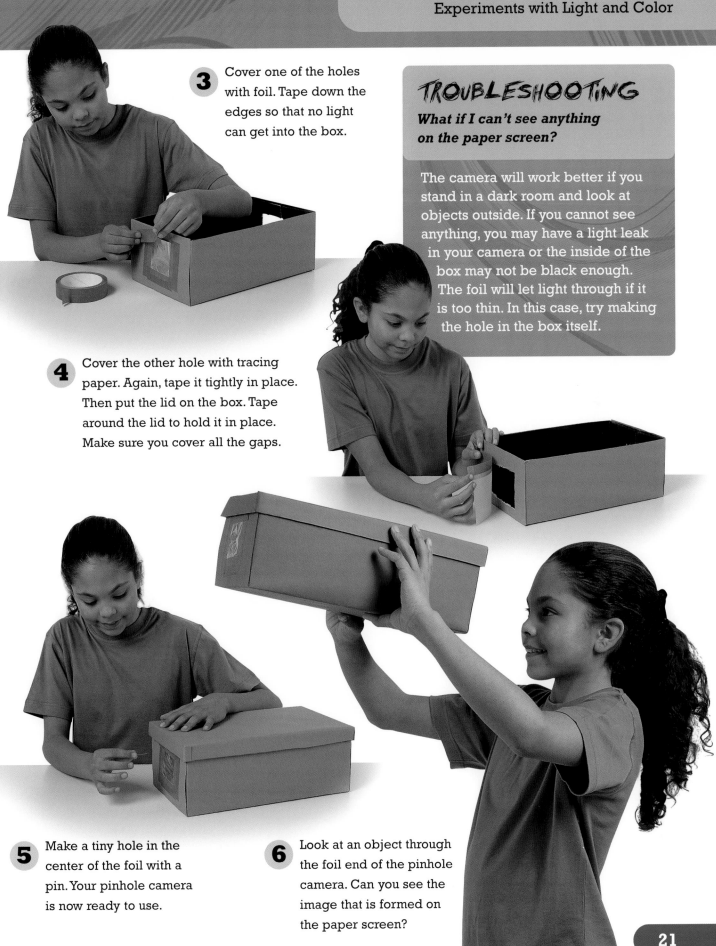

3 Cover one of the holes with foil. Tape down the edges so that no light can get into the box.

TROUBLESHOOTING

What if I can't see anything on the paper screen?

The camera will work better if you stand in a dark room and look at objects outside. If you cannot see anything, you may have a light leak in your camera or the inside of the box may not be black enough. The foil will let light through if it is too thin. In this case, try making the hole in the box itself.

4 Cover the other hole with tracing paper. Again, tape it tightly in place. Then put the lid on the box. Tape around the lid to hold it in place. Make sure you cover all the gaps.

5 Make a tiny hole in the center of the foil with a pin. Your pinhole camera is now ready to use.

6 Look at an object through the foil end of the pinhole camera. Can you see the image that is formed on the paper screen?

Spectrometer

What you will need

- shoebox
- scissors
- tape
- construction paper
- thin mesh window screen
- lens
- flashlight
- colored pencils
- white paper
- modeling clay

Goals

1 Show that light travels in waves.

2 Use your spectrometer to make a spectrum.

LEVEL of Difficulty

 Hard   Medium   Easy

1 Cut a hole in each end of the shoebox, about 2 inches (5cm) square. Stick two pieces of construction paper over one hole. Leave a narrow vertical slit to let light into the box.

2 Cut three pieces of mesh window screen to fit over the other hole in the box. Overlap the pieces. Tape them in place on the box.

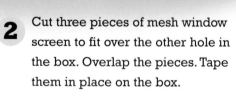

TROUBLESHOOTING

What if there's no spectrum?

If you cannot see a spectrum, turn the mesh around by a quarter turn. It might also help to tape around the lid of the shoebox to keep light from leaking in. If there's still no spectrum, widen the slit a little or use a brighter flashlight. Closing the curtains and turning out the lights will help you see the spectrum.

3 Put the lid on the box. You now have a spectrometer! Shine a light into the slit, and hold the lens in front of the mesh. Place the white paper on the table. A spectrum should appear on it.

DIFFRACTION GRATING

Use a commercial diffraction grating instead of window screen if you can get one. The stores in some science museums sometimes sell diffraction gratings. Your science teacher might also be able to lend you one.

4 Hold the lens in place with a piece of clay. Copy the spectrum onto the white paper with colored pencils.

23

Making Moiré Patterns

Goals

1 Make your own swirling moiré patterns.

2 Compare moiré patterns made by straight lines to patterns made by circles.

LEVEL of Difficulty

 Hard   Medium   Easy

What you will need

- two small combs
- thin pen
- paper
- ruler
- access to photocopier and transparencies
- thin mesh window screen

SHOW ME THE MONEY

Look closely at a dollar bill. You will see patterns of circles printed on the paper. These patterns make it difficult for criminals to copy the bills. A moiré pattern appears if a criminal uses a color photocopier to copy the bill. So it is obvious the copy is a fake.

1 Hold the combs in front of a light source, such as a table lamp. Slowly move one in front of the other. Can you see patterns of lines (not the teeth of the combs)?

SAFETY TIP !

Do not use the Sun as your source of light in this experiment. Looking directly at the Sun can damage your eyes.

TROUBLESHOOTING

How do I draw concentric circles?

The easiest way to draw concentric circles is to use a drawing program on a computer. Draw a large circle, copy and paste it over the first, and then reduce the diameter of the circle a bit. Continue until you've filled the space inside the largest circle. You could also use a pair of compasses and a pen to draw the circles on tracing paper.

2 Draw a pattern of concentric circles (circles inside each other) on white paper. Photocopy this pattern onto two transparencies. Overlap them to make moiré patterns.

3 Slide two pieces of window screen over each other. Watch moiré patterns appear within them.

The moiré pattern on the left was made by overlapping two sets of straight lines.

Sunset in a Glass

What you will need

- large glass
- water
- milk
- powerful flashlight
- plastic sheets of different colors

Goals

1 Scatter light through a glass of milky water.

2 Find out which colors scatter most easily.

LEVEL of Difficulty

 Hard

 Medium

 Easy

VOLCANIC SUNSETS

The most dramatic sunsets happen after a volcano erupts. Ash from the volcano rises high into the air. The tiny particles of ash scatter red light. This makes the sky around the Sun much redder than usual.

1 Fill the glass with water. Add a little milk.

2 Shine the flashlight through one side of the glass. Look at the beam of light through the glass. Look all around the glass to see the beam from all angles.

TROUBLESHOOTING

What if I can't see the beam?

Use the most powerful flashlight you can find. Check the batteries if the beam seems weak. Make sure you don't put too much milk in the water, because this would block the beam completely. It will also help if you turn out the lights and close the drapes when you do this experiment.

3 Shine the flashlight through a colored plastic sheet and through the glass. Look through the glass from all around again. Does the beam of light look any different?

RED SKY AT NIGHT

Sometimes the sky turns red just before the Sun rises or just after the Sun sets. This occurs when Earth's atmosphere bends sunlight from below the horizon.

4 Try the experiment using sheets of different colors. Write down what you see for each color.

Separating Colors

Goals

1 See how to separate different chemicals.

2 Practice paper chromatography.

LEVEL of Difficulty Hard Medium Easy

What you will need

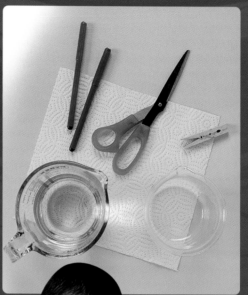

- white paper towel
- scissors
- glass measuring cup
- glass beaker or cup
- water
- 2 washable felt-tip pens of different colors
- clothes pin

2 Pour about 1 inch (2.5cm) of water into the glass beaker or cup.

1 Cut a strip of white paper towel about 4 inches (10cm) long and 1 inch (2.5cm) wide.

3 Draw two dots of different colors about 2 inches (5cm) from the end of the strip. Make the dots about the same size.

4 Use a clothes pin to attach the strip of paper towel onto the edge of the beaker. The end with the two dots should just be touching the water.

COLORED CANDIES

Brightly colored candies contain food coloring that is water soluble, so you can try crushing some candy into a dish and mixing it with warm water. Place a drop of this solution onto the paper towel, and wait to see the colors that separate out.

5 The water will gradually move up the paper towel, taking the chemicals that make up the colors of each dot with it. You may be surprised by the hidden colors that appear!

TROUBLESHOOTING

What if the colors did not separate?

Repeat the experiment with different colors. Black works well because it is made of lots of different colors. Don't use light colors, such as pink or yellow, because they are hard to see. Also, make sure that you use washable pens. Only water-based dyes will dissolve in the water.

Glossary

artificial lights: lights that are manmade and not natural. Artificial lights are used in many forms, from lighting in homes and buildings to traffic lights on the street.

atmosphere: the envelope of gas that surrounds a planet. Earth's atmosphere is known as the air.

crest: the top of a wave

diffraction: spreading out in waves

eclipse: when the Sun is blocked from view and its light is blocked from Earth. An eclipse is caused when the Moon passes between Earth and the Sun.

gamma ray: a form of light that has the smallest wavelength of any light form. Gamma rays are made by radioactivity.

infrared: a form of light created by electromagnetic rays. We cannot see infrared light, but it can be felt as heat.

lens: a piece of glass that helps people to see objects far away or close up. A concave lens is thinner in the middle and makes objects look smaller. A convex lens is thicker in the middle and makes objects look bigger.

microscope: a device that has several lenses which make tiny objects look thousands of times bigger than they really are. Microscopes are used to see tiny objects that are not visible to the naked human eye.

optic nerve: a nerve inside the eye that sends messages from the eye to the brain

particles: tiniest known objects

plankton: a tiny animal that can only be seen under a microscope. Plankton are eaten by some whales and other sea creatures.

prism: a transparent, usually glass, shape used to separate light into colors

radiation: an energy given off by sources. Heat and light are forms of radiation.

reflection: light "bounced" back off the surface of water, glass, metal, and so on

refraction: when light changes direction as it passes through water, glass, and air

solar energy: energy that is created by the Sun. Solar energy can be used to heat and light buildings and power machines.

spectrometer: a machine that studies light

spectrum: when white light passes through a prism and produces a rainbow of colors. The rainbow is the spectrum.

telescope: a device that uses many lenses to make distant objects look much bigger

transparent: see-through

trough: the lowest part of a wave

ultraviolet: a form of light created by electromagnetic rays, but which cannot be seen

wavelength: distance between the crests of a wave

X-ray: a process that uses electromagnetic radiation to pass tiny particles through the body to create images of the internal features. The images are then stored by a computer.

Further Information

BOOKS

Parker, Steve. *The Science of Light: Projects and Experiments with Light and Color.* Mankato, MN: Heinemann-Raintree, 2005.

Tocci, Salvatore. *Experiments with Light.* New York: Children's Press, 2002.

Trumbauer, Lisa. *All About Light.* New York: Children's Press, 2004.

WEBSITES

www.light-science.com/agesto12.html

www.opticalres.com/kidoptx_f.html

www.learner.org/teacherslab/science/light

Index